THE BIBLE
JESUS
READ

By Philip Yancey

The Jesus I Never Knew

What's So Amazing about Grace?

The Bible Jesus Read

Reaching for the Invisible God

Where Is God When It Hurts?

Disappointment with God

The Student Bible, General Edition (with Tim Stafford)

Meet the Bible (with Brenda Quinn)

Church: Why Bother?

Finding God in Unexpected Places

I Was Just Wondering

Soul Survivor

Rumors of Another World

Prayer: Does It Make Any Difference?

By Philip Yancey and Dr. Paul Brand

Fearfully and Wonderfully Made

In His Image

The Gift of Pain

In the Likeness of God

PHILIP YANCEY

with

Stephen and Amanda Sorenson

THE BIBLE JESUS READ

Particpant's Guide

An 8-Session Exploration of the Old Testament

ZONDERVAN®

ZONDERVAN.com/
AUTHORTRACKER
follow your favorite authors

The Bible Jesus Read Participant's Guide
Copyright © 2002 by Philip D. Yancey

Requests for information should be addressed to:

Zondervan, Grand Rapids, Michigan 49530

ISBN-10: 0-310-24185-5
ISBN-13: 978-0-310-24185-0

Interior design by Todd Sprague

Printed in the United States of America

11 12 13 • 31 30 29 28 27 26 25 24 23 22 21 20 19 18 17

CONTENTS

CONTENTS

PREFACE

I have met many Christians who have only read the New Testament, not the Old. They may have tried to read the Old Testament here and there, but they found it too long, too disordered, or simply too strange. I sympathize, but at the same time I feel sad for those people because I don't think we get a full picture of how a life with God works from the New Testament alone.

The book I wrote, which we are studying here, is titled *The Bible Jesus Read* because, when you think about it, Jesus didn't have Paul's Epistles or the Gospels. So when he would go away and spend time meditating on God's Word, he used the Psalms, the Prophets, the books of Moses. That's where Jesus believed his relationship with God the Father was formed and examined.

When I meet people who tell me they were bored by or had a hard time reading the Old Testament, I say, "Welcome to the club!" It takes work. The Old Testament is a long book, and parts of it are slow. What I have found, though, is that the more work you put into it the more you'll get out of it. This Participant's Guide and accompanying materials in this Zondervan *Groupware*™ curriculum will give you a set of tools and approaches that will help you interpret the Old Testament and appropriate its wisdom.

I find it is helpful for me just to remember what the Old Testament is. The Old Testament is God's living message to us. It consists of truths he wants us to know about himself, about us, and about life.

The effort and commitment you put into your study of the Old Testament—including these Zondervan *Groupware* sessions—will yield a richness and value I believe you cannot obtain from any other source. This is, after all, the Bible Jesus read.

Philip Yancey

Is the Old Testament Worth the Effort?

Apart from the Old Testament, we will always have an impoverished view of God. God is not a philosophical construct but a Person who acts in history: the one who created Adam, who gave a promise to Noah, who called Abraham and introduced himself by name to Moses, who deigned to live in a wilderness *tent* in order to live close to his people. From Genesis 1 onward, God has wanted himself to be known, and the Old Testament is our most complete revelation of what God is like.

—Philip Yancey

Questions to Think About

1. When you hear the words "Old Testament," what thoughts and feelings come to mind?

2. What personal challenges have you faced when you have tried to read and understand the Old Testament?

3. What have you enjoyed about your ventures into the Old Testament, and what might be some of the benefits of becoming more familiar with it?

Video Presentation: "Is the Old Testament Worth the Effort?"

God wants us to know about him

What Jesus read

Why read the Old Testament?

Discomfort is not bad

Honest feelings

Video Highlights

1. If the New Testament doesn't give a complete picture of what God wants us to know about him, what do you hope to learn from the Old Testament?

Discovering the Old Testament

There is so much of benefit for us to discover in the Old Testament. If only we would read it, we would:

- Gain a better understanding of the Old Testament concepts and allusions found in Hebrews, Jude, Revelation, and other New Testament books.
- Begin uncovering the layers of richness in the Epistles and Gospels that shed light backward on the Old Testament.
- Understand more about what God is really like and how he has worked—and is working—in the lives of his people.
- Benefit from the lessons of faith discovered by ancient Old Testament heroes.
- Have a richer, deeper understanding of the redemptive love story between God and his people that continues to unfold today.
- Begin to grasp the degree to which what we say, how we behave, and even what we think and feel influences God and how much he delights in us.
- Learn the lessons of faith—faith that is entirely human, yet rock-solid—that sustained so many Old Testament characters and can sustain us when we face life's challenges.

2. Which thoughts and emotions began to surface as you watched this video? What surprised you or stood out above the rest?

3. Philip Yancey spoke of the relevance and realism of the Old Testament. What hope does the graphic realism of the Old Testament offer you in relationship to your walk with God?

Large Group Exploration: Why Read the Old Testament?

Years ago most people knew at least something about the Old Testament—the story of David and Goliath, some of the Ten Commandments, or the story of Noah. Today, however, knowledge of the Old Testament is fading fast among Christians and has virtually vanished in popular culture. Let's consider some of the challenges to and benefits of reading the Old Testament.

Perspective

The Old Testament is not, as one theologian suggested, "reading someone else's mail"; it is our mail as well. The people who appear in it were real people learning to get along with the same God that I worship. I need to learn from their experience even as I try to incorporate the marvelous new message brought by Jesus.

—Philip Yancey

1. It's easy to think that we *ought* to read the Old Testament and therefore lump it into the same category as other things we *should* do—floss our teeth, exercise regularly, eat right, or listen more attentively to a spouse. In what ways have you felt obligated to read the Old Testament? If you have ever attempted to read through the Bible, such as in a "Read the Bible in a Year" program, how did it work out?

2. From the reading or study you have done, describe the ways in which you have found the God featured in the Old Testament to be similar to or different from the God featured in the New Testament.

3. As he walked along the road to Emmaus, Jesus explained to two of his grieving disciples "what was said in all the Scriptures concerning himself" (Luke 24:27). What does this tell us about Jesus' view of the Old Testament Scriptures? What does it reveal about his love for, commitment to, and understanding of the Old Testament?

4. What unique perspectives on our relationship with God—including our doubts, struggles, and pain—might the Old Testament provide?

Jesus Knew His Bible Well

Jesus often referred to the Old Testament writings and pointed out important facts about himself and his mission. The following chart reveals some of the times when Jesus quoted directly from the Old Testament.

Situation	What Jesus Said
Matthew 13:13–15; Mark 4:12	Isaiah 6:9–10
Mark 7:6–7	Isaiah 29:13
Mark 7:10	Exodus 20:12; 21:17; Leviticus 20:9; Deuteronomy 5:16
Mark 9:48	Isaiah 66:24
Mark 11:17	Isaiah 56:7
Luke 4:4	Deuteronomy 8:3
Luke 4:8	Deuteronomy 6:13
Luke 4:10–11	Psalm 91:11–12
Luke 4:12	Deuteronomy 6:16
Luke 4:18–19	Isaiah 61:1–2
Luke 7:27	Malachi 3:1
Luke 10:27	Deuteronomy 6:5
Luke 18:20	Exodus 20:12–16; Deuteronomy 5:16–20
Luke 20:17	Psalm 118:22
John 6:31	Exodus 16:4; Nehemiah 9:15
John 13:18	Psalm 41:9

Small Group Exploration: Opening the Curtain on a Bigger Picture of God

The Old Testament reveals a rich picture of what God—the personal God who loves us and wants to be in relationship with us—is like. Let's break into groups of three to five and look at a few "snapshots" of what the Old Testament reveals about God and his relationship with us.

1. What imagery did David use to describe God's care for his people? In what ways is this like or unlike the New Testament image of God? (See Psalm 17:8–9; 57:1; 91:1–4.)

2. What does Isaiah 62:2–5 reveal about God's desire and love for his people? To what does he compare his relationship to his people? What is your response to these expressions of honor and delight?

3. What imagery is used in Isaiah 40:9–11 to show God's love for his people?

4. The Old Testament records times when God allowed people to exert an influence on him as well as times when he exerted his influence on them. Discuss what happened in the following situations, particularly in terms of the relationship between God and his people.

   a. Genesis 18:22–33

   b. 1 Samuel 7:2–10

5. God wanted the ancient Hebrews to continually remind themselves that the world revolved around God, not themselves. Look up the following verses and describe what God commanded the Israelites to do in order to stay focused on him.

   a. Exodus 13:1–16

   b. Numbers 15:37–41

Perspective

I've met a lot of Christians who have only read the New Testament. They may have tried the Old Testament here or there, and found it a little off-putting and just gave up. I feel sad for those Christians, frankly, because I don't think we get a full picture of how a life with God works from the New Testament.

—Philip Yancey

Group Discussion

1. The Old Testament is a timeless, inspired message given to us by God that tells us what God wants us to know—about him, about life, and about ourselves. In what ways has what we have seen and discussed together today influenced your view of the Old Testament?

2. The Old Testament gives us an advanced course in life with God and, in so doing, expands our concept of God and helps deepen our relationship with him. Take a few minutes to consider your personal relationship with God in light of what you have explored today.

Personal Journey: To Begin Now

No wonder those of us who have grown up with abstract concepts of God find it confusing to try to make logical sense out of the Old Testament! The Old Testament presents laws and history, but it also speaks to us in images of a God and Creator who desires to be in close relationship with us.

Take some time now by yourself to consider what you have discovered in this session and how it applies to your daily life.

Read Deuteronomy 6:1–12.

1. What kind of a relationship does this passage indicate God wants to have with his people?

2. What was God's overarching concern about his relationship with his people? What things did God want his people to do in order to preserve their relationship with him?

3. Jesus considered the command to "love the Lord your God with all
   your heart and with all your soul and with all your strength" to be
   the essential commandment. What can you incorporate into your
   daily life that will help you obey this commandment?

Did You Know?

Unlike many Christians today, the New Testament Christians eagerly
pursued the Old Testament Scriptures. They found in the Old Testament a wealth of understanding about the kind of relationship God
desired to have with them. Paul, for example, constantly referred to
the Old Testament in his writings. Note the many Old Testament
connections that appear in the third chapter of Galatians alone!

Galatians 3	Old Testament Connections
v. 6 Mentions Abraham's belief	Genesis 15:6
v. 8 Mentions God's promise to bless all nations through Abraham	Genesis 12:3; 18:18; 22:18
v. 10 Quotes from the Old Testament Law	Deuteronomy 27:26
v. 11 Quotes from an Old Testament prophet	Habbakuk 2:4
v. 12 References the Old Testament Law	Leviticus 18:5
v. 13 Quotes an Old Testament verse	Deuteronomy 21:23
v. 16 Analyzes several Old Testament references	Genesis 12:7; 13:15; and 24:7

Personal Journey: To Do between Sessions

Set aside at least one hour away from distractions to do the following exercise.

1. Take an inventory of what you believe about the Old Testament. List your likes and dislikes, the things that confuse or excite you, your favorite passages, etc. Be sure to include at least two ways in which you might benefit from further exploration of the Old Testament.

2. Write down some ways in which you might be able to use the above "inventory" to chart a new approach toward the Old Testament. For example, if you tend to be bored by all the history in the Bible, you may want to reread portions of it through the lens of a specific perspective. Instead of focusing on the violence or trying to follow the historic sequence, you may want to look for insight into God's character or look for evidence of his desire for relationship.

Perspective

It may prove dangerous to get involved with the Bible. You approach it with a series of questions, and as you enter it you find the questions turned back upon you. King David got swept up in a story by the prophet Nathan and leaped to his feet indignant—only to learn the barbed story concerned himself. I find something similar at work again and again as I read the Old Testament. I am thrown back on what I truly believe. I am forced to reexamine. . . . After spending time exploring the Old Testament, I can truthfully say that I come away more astonished, not less.

—Philip Yancey

3. Begin reading the Old Testament. Consider how much of an invest-
ment you want to make in exploring the Old Testament and set a goal
for yourself. If you get bogged down in a difficult area, feel free to
take a refreshing break by going to one of your favorite Old Testament passages then approaching the more difficult passage again
later, or, choose a new passage.

Two-Week Old Testament Reading Plan

The Student Bible has a two-week Old Testament reading plan that
provides an overview of Old Testament highlights. If you are just
beginning to study the Old Testament, it's a good way to start.

Day 1: Genesis 1—The story of Creation
Day 2: Genesis 3—The origin of sin
Day 3: Genesis 22—Abraham and Isaac
Day 4: Exodus 3—Moses' encounter with God
Day 5: Exodus 20—The gift of the Ten Commandments
Day 6: 1 Samuel 13—David and Goliath
Day 7: 2 Samuel 11—David and Bathsheba
Day 8: 2 Samuel 12—Nathan's rebuke of the king
Day 9: 1 Kings 18—Elijah and the prophets of Baal
Day 10: Job 38—God's answer to Job
Day 11: Psalm 51—A classic confession
Day 12: Isaiah 40—Words of comfort from God
Day 13: Daniel 6—Daniel and the lions
Day 14: Amos 4—A prophet's stern warning

Understanding the Old Testament

The Old Testament is the story of the tremendous decline—very quickly—of what God had created. It relates his slow, tedious progress to create a people, and out of that people to send his Son, who would take the same message of God's love and introduce it to all the nations of the world.

—Philip Yancey

Questions to Think About

1. Think about the Old Testament reading you have done in the past. Which themes stand out to you?

2. What relationships do you see between these themes? In what ways do these relationships indicate the existence of a "bigger picture"?

3. If you were to make the Old Testament into a movie, what might you choose as the story line or plot?

Video Presentation: "Understanding the Old Testament"

The Old Testament, a single, coherent story

The Old Testament plot:
A discouraging beginning

God's new plan

God's vision is fulfilled, then fades

The prophets remind the people of God's vision

Four hundred years of silence

Jesus: a new messenger, a new kind of relationship

Video Highlights

1. Philip said, "I would express the plot like this: God creates a world and a family. He loses that family, and then he gets it back." How well does this plot match what you know of the Old Testament? In what ways does it help you to better understand the Old Testament?

2. What role does Jesus' coming to earth after a silence of four hundred years play in the Old Testament's plot? What does this event tell us about God?

Perspective

The Bible's striking unity is one strong sign that God directed its composition. By using a variety of authors and cultural situations, God developed a complete record of what he wants us to know; amazingly, the parts fit together in such a way that a single story does emerge.

—Philip Yancey

Large Group Exploration: Old Testament Overview

Our exploration time today will differ from what we did in our previous session. We're going to remain together as a large group to consider a few key highlights of the plot of the Old Testament's story. So hold onto your seats, because we have about twenty minutes to give ourselves an overview of the entire Old Testament!

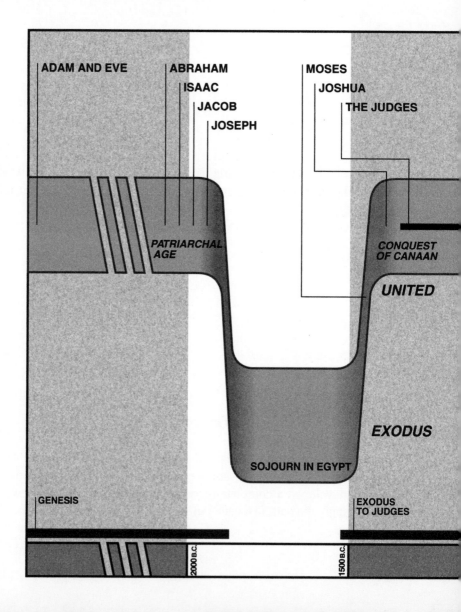

Perspective

The Old Testament . . . does not give us a lesson in theology, with abstract concepts neatly arranged in logical order. Quite the opposite: it gives an advanced course in Life with God, expressed in a style at once personal and passionate.

—Philip Yancey

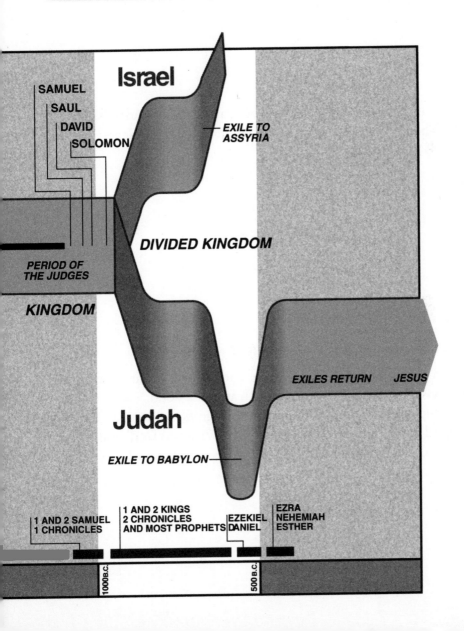

God Creates a World

1. What did God have in mind for his human creation at the beginning, and what response did he receive? (See Genesis 1:27; 2:15–18; 3:1–11.)

2. As Adam's family grew, what kind of relationship did Adam's descendants have with God? What was God's response? (See Genesis 6:5–8; 7:1–4; 8:15–19.)

God Chooses a Family to Fulfill His New Plan

3. Noah had three sons—Shem, Ham, and Japheth—who fathered the nations that spread out over the earth after the flood. One of Shem's descendants was Abram, an otherwise insignificant nomad. But God singled out Abram and appeared to him. What was God's message to Abram? What was Abram's response? (See Genesis 12:1–8.)

4. God had chosen a family to carry out his plan, but the road to fulfilling that plan was bumpy indeed. The chart below highlights a few of the high points and low points. Review the chart and discuss what you would have thought God was doing at various points along the way. At which times might you have thought God had given up on his plan? At which times might you have thought God's plan was near fulfillment? Which other low and high points of Old Testament history prior to the Exodus stand out in your mind? As you see the Old Testament story unfold, what are your thoughts about God?

Reference	Low Point	High Point
Genesis 15:2–6	Sarah, Abram's wife, was barren	
Genesis 17:15–17; 21:1–7		In her old age, Sarah gave birth to Isaac
Genesis 22:1–2	God asked Abram to sacrifice Isaac	
Genesis 22:13		God provided a ram as a substitute sacrifice for Isaac
Genesis 32:28; 35:23–26; 49:1		Isaac's son, Jacob, had twelve sons who were to father the twelve tribes of Israel
Genesis 37:23–36	Jacob's ten oldest sons sold their brother Joseph as a slave and convinced Jacob that Joseph was dead	

Genesis 41:41–43; 42:1–2; 45:4–7		Joseph became second in command in Egypt and was able to save his family from starvation
Exodus 1:6–7		The Israelites prospered in Egypt
Exodus 1:8–14	The Egyptians eventually forgot who Joseph was and enslaved the Israelites	
Exodus 2:1–10; 3:1–10		After 430 years, God raised up Moses to bring God's people out of Egypt

God's Covenant with His People

5. What kinds of challenges did the Israelites face as they traversed the wilderness after leaving Egypt? How did they respond? How did God respond? (See Exodus 16:1–3, 11–16; 17:1–6, 8–13.)

6. Three months to the day after leaving Egypt, the Israelites camped at the foot of Mount Sinai.

   a. What message did God give to Moses and his people? (See Exodus 19:1–6.)

b. How did the people respond to God's offer by their *words* and by their *actions?* (See Exodus 24:3; 32:1–4.)

c. What was God's response to their sin? (See Exodus 32:9–14.)

Life in the Promised Land

7. After accepting God's covenant, the people continued their journey toward Canaan. Yet, just as before, they continued to struggle with unfaithfulness, disobedience, and grumbling. Their history in receiving and settling the land God promised to them fits a "bad news, good news" pattern.

   By this point, God had made known his desire for his chosen people. Review the following chart and discuss how you think God viewed each of these circumstances. At which points would you have thought God would have given up on his plan? What does this "bad news, good news" pattern reveal to you about the heart of God?

Reference	Bad News	Good News
Numbers 13:17–30		The land of Canaan was abundantly fertile
Numbers 13:31–14:24	The people were so afraid of the giants living in Canaan's fortified cities that they wanted to stone the Isrealite leaders and go back to Egypt, which led to forty years of desert wandering	
Joshua 3:1, 5–16; 4:19–24		By God's miraculous power, the people crossed the Jordan River into Canaan
Joshua 24:11–24		Under Joshua's leadership, the people promised to serve and obey the Lord only
Judges 2:6–7, 10–15	The next generation abandoned God and worshiped the gods of the Canaanites, so God allowed their enemies to oppress them	
Judges 2:16, 18		God raised up judges to save and lead his people
Judges 2:17, 19	After each judge died, the people went back to their evil ways	
1 Samuel 8:4–20; 11:15; 12:19–20	Despite God's warnings, the people rejected God as their king and Saul became king	
1 Samuel 13:6–14	Saul disobeyed God, so God chose another person to be king	
1 Samuel 16:1, 6–13		Samuel anointed David, the Lord's choice for a new king

2 Samuel 5:1–7; 7:8–16		David united the nation and captured Zion (Jerusalem), and God promised that David's house would endure forever
2 Samuel 11:2–17	David stumbled, committing adultery and murder	
2 Samuel 12:1–14		Nathan confronted David with his sin and David repented
1 Kings 3:7–14; 6:1, 8; 9:1–9		Solomon became king, asked God for wisdom, and built a beautiful temple for God
1 Kings 11:1–6; 9–13	Solomon married many foreign wives who turned his heart away from God	
1 Kings 12:1–5; 12–19	Rehoboam succeeds Solomon, but the kingdom splits under his harsh rule	

The Cry of the Prophets

8. Almost immediately after Israel defected from Rehoboam's rule, its rulers encouraged the people to pursue evil and worship idols (1 Kings 12:26–30). King Ahab, who married Jezebel (a practicing witch and Phoenician princess), was the culmination of this evil line of kings. After Ahab built a temple to Baal (1 Kings 16:30–33), God could take no more and responded to Ahab's flagrant sinfulness. Who did God send to ask the people to choose whether they belonged to God or to Baal? What was the result? (See 1 Kings 18:15–40; 19:14–18.)

9. The spiritual condition of Israel, the northern kingdom, continued to deteriorate, so God sent prophets such as Amos and Hosea to try to turn his chosen family back to him. Ironically, God used the nation that had listened to Jonah—Assyria—to destroy stubborn Israel in the end. Prophets such as Joel, Isaiah, Micah, Habakkuk, Jeremiah, and Ezekiel spoke God's words to the people of Judah, in the south, who also grew more and more unfaithful to God. Finally, what did God allow King Nebuchadnezzar of Babylon to do? (See 2 Kings 25:8–21.)

10. Even while God's people were in exile, Satan was working to destroy God's plan. The book of Esther exposes yet another attack by Satan against God's chosen family. What was the threat, and how was it resolved? (See Esther 3:5–14; 8:3–8, 11.)

11. Such Old Testament books as Ezra, Haggai, and Zechariah record what happened to the Jews after their return to Jerusalem from captivity. Malachi, the last prophet recorded in the Old Testament, saw that the Jews in Judah doubted God's love for them, questioned his justice, and were content to pursue evil (Malachi 1:2; 2:10–12; 3:5–7, 13–14). He spoke out prophetically, but for the most part was ignored. So for four hundred years God was silent, until he brought his plan of redemption into being. What do you notice in Matthew 1 in light of the study we've just done? (Note particularly verses 1 and 17.)

The Old Testament Points to Jesus!

The Old Testament has many prophecies of a coming Messiah that were fulfilled by Jesus.

Prophecy of a Coming Messiah	Fulfillment by Jesus
Would descend from the tribe of Judah (Genesis 49:10)	He descended from the tribe of Judah (Luke 3:33)
Would be heir to the throne of David (Isaiah 9:7)	He was in the lineage of David (Matthew 1:1, 6)
Would be born in Bethlehem (Micah 5:2)	He was born in Bethlehem (Matthew 2:1)
Daniel tells when the "Anointed One" would come (Daniel 9:25)	He was born during the days of Caesar Augustus (Luke 2:1–2)
Would be born of a virgin (Isaiah 7:14)	He was born of a virgin (Matthew 1:18)
Would minister in Galilee (Isaiah 9:1–2)	He ministered in Galilee (Matthew 4:12–16)
Would be a prophet (Deuteronomy 18:15)	He was a prophet (John 6:14)
Would enter triumphantly into Jerusalem (Zechariah 9:9)	He entered Jerusalem triumphantly (John 12:12–15)
Would be betrayed by a friend (Psalm 41:9)	He was betrayed by Judas (Mark 14:10)
Would be sold for thirty pieces of silver (Zechariah 11:13)	He was sold by Judas for thirty pieces of silver (Matthew 26:15)
Would be struck and spit upon (Isaiah 50:6)	Jews struck him and spit upon him (Mark 14:65; John 19:1–3)
Soldiers would cast lots for his clothes (Psalm 22:18)	Soldiers cast lots for his clothes (Mark 15:24)
Would be resurrected from the dead (Psalm 16:10)	He was resurrected from the dead (Matthew 28:5–9; Luke 24:36–48)
Would ascend to heaven (Psalm 68:18)	He ascended to heaven (Luke 24:50–51)

Group Discussion

1. As you've seen a little bit of the Old Testament story unfold, what new things are you seeing in the Old Testament that you have not seen before?

2. In what ways do you better understand Philip Yancey's summation of the Old Testament's story line: "God creates a world and a family. He loses that family, and then he gets it back"?

Did You Know?

I find it remarkable that this diverse collection of manuscripts written over a period of a millennium by several dozen authors possesses as much unity as it does. To appreciate this feat, imagine a book begun five hundred years before Columbus and just now completed!

—Philip Yancey

Personal Journey: To Begin Now

When we begin to see how the Old Testament story unfolds, God's message to us becomes more understandable. Through the trials and tribulations and ups and downs of God's family, we see recurring themes of sin and repentance, forgiveness and judgment, hope and sorrow, joy and despair. We discover a greater understanding of God's love for us—a fuller picture of his mercy and patient longsuffering.

Take some time by yourself to consider what you have discovered in this session and how it applies to your daily life.

1. Write a short, personal summary of how your understanding of the Old Testament or the God of the Old Testament has grown today. If you aren't sure how to start, use the following questions as a guide:

   In what ways do you feel you know God better now than when you got up this morning?

   What did you learn about God that awed or surprised you today?

   How would you describe the Old Testament story in a sentence or two?

   What surprised you about what you discovered today?

Summary:

Perspective

When I see God working with individual human beings, it's amazing what he puts up with. God can take anything as long as his people turn back to him and let him pick them up. We fall down, we get up. We fall down, we get up. All the way through the Old Testament I see pictures of that grace. God forgives. He gives people a new start. That God of mercy and grace shines all the way through the Old Testament.

—Philip Yancey

2. As you consider the ups and downs of the Old Testament history of God's chosen people, what messages do you find that are relevant to you? In what ways do you see your relationship with God reflected in the Old Testament stories? How might that affect your relationship with God from now on?

Personal Journey: To Do between Sessions

As the title of Philip's book expresses, the Old Testament *is* the Bible Jesus read. He prayed its prayers. Memorized its poems. Sang its songs. Heard its stories. Pondered its prophecies. He also used phrases from the Old Testament to define himself and traced in its passages every important fact about himself and his mission. The more we comprehend the Old Testament, the more we comprehend him.

1. In what ways has your understanding of who Jesus is and what he came to earth to accomplish grown as a result of this session?

2. What will you do to draw closer to the God who reveals himself through the pages of the Old Testament?

3. Take a look at the charts provided for Questions 4 and 7 of your Large Group Exploration time. To gain a deeper understanding of exactly what occurred, read the passages indicated. As you read, take particular note of the interaction between God and his people and the responses of both.

Job: Seeing in the Dark

Job does in fact focus on the problem of suffering, but in a most unexpected way. It brilliantly asks the questions we most urgently want answered, then turns aside to propose another way of looking at the problem entirely. Like most of the Old Testament, Job at first frustrates, by refusing the simple answers we think we want, and then oddly satisfies, by pointing us in a new direction marked by flagrant realism and a tantalizing glimpse of hope.

—Philip Yancey

Questions to Think About

1. What words first come to mind when someone mentions the book of Job?

2. In what ways have you felt like Job? How do you respond to God when you can't figure out why God is allowing hard times in your life or in the life of someone you love? In what ways do you find it easy or difficult to be honest with God about your thoughts and feelings?

3. How do you think God views our suffering?

Video Presentation: "Job: Seeing in the Dark"

What's the real question?

Who is really on trial?

The question of faith: Can this be turned into good?

Living honestly with unanswered questions

How we respond to our distress matters to God

Video Highlights

1. In what ways has this video challenged your thinking on why bad things happen to good people? Explain why you agree or disagree with Philip Yancey's conclusion that how we respond to suffering is the real issue.

2. One of Philip Yancey's conclusions from the book of Job is that "God cares more about our faith than our pleasure." How do you respond to that conclusion, and what are its implications for your life?

Large Group Exploration: Peeking "Behind the Curtain" as Job's Story Unfolds

Philip Yancey found it helpful to think of the book of Job as a mystery play, a "whodunit" detective story. "We in the audience have showed up early for a press conference in which the director explains his work (chapters 1–2)," he writes. "We learn in advance who did what in the play, and we understand that the personal drama on earth has its origin in a cosmic drama in heaven—the contest over Job's faith."

As Job's story unfolds, we—the audience—know the answers. We know that Job isn't being punished. We know that God is using him to prove to Satan that a human being's faith can be genuine and selfless. We know everything—except how Job will respond. The actors in the play, however, have no knowledge of what's to come or why things are happening. Like many other Old Testament stories, their stories reveal much about God and what it means to be a human being in relationship with God. Let's quickly review this story and see what we discover.

The Contest between Satan and God

God's Position	Satan's Challenge
God is worthy of love simply because of who he is, not what he does. People follow him because they love him, not because they are "bribed" to do so.	Job loves God only because he receives blessings from God. God is not worthy of love in himself.
Job has faith in God apart from God's blessings.	Job will abandon his "faith" in God as soon as the blessings disappear.
Job's faith is not a result of environmental manipulation. He will choose to believe in God despite what happens to him.	Human beings are not really free to believe, to exercise faith in God. Faith is just a product of environment and circumstances.

1. Read the following passages from Job 1–2 and note what each reveals about the main characters and plot of the drama that unfolds.

   a. What do we know about Job? (See Job 1:1–5.)

   b. What do we know about Satan, his argument with God, and the results? (See Job 1:6–12; 2:1–7.)

   c. What bad things happened to Job? (See Job 1:13–22; 2:7–10.)

   d. Who came to be with Job, and what was their initial response? (See Job 2:11–13.)

Perspective

Job prefers to live with an agonizing paradox, that God still loves him even though all evidence points against it. His friends laid out the logic: *Suffering comes from God. God is just. Therefore you, Job, are guilty.* After examining his own life, and toying with the notion of an unjust God, Job arrives at a different formula that on the surface makes no sense: *Suffering comes from God. God is just. I am innocent.* In the best Hebrew tradition, Job clings to all three of those truths no matter how contradictory they seem.

—Philip Yancey

2. Finally, God swept onto the "stage" of Job's story and, in the last five chapters of the book (Job 38–42), presented his "answer" to Job's questions and accusations.

   a. Describe the theme of God's message and Job's response to his long-awaited, face-to-face encounter with God. (See Job 38:1–3; 40:1–7; 42:1–6.)

   b. What did God conclude about the arguments of Job's friends? (See Job 42:7–9.)

Small Group Exploration: A Test of Faith

The real issue explored in the book of Job is whether a human being will trust a sovereign, invisible God even when circumstances do not support that trust. All of us at times find ourselves in a Job-like state. We may not face disasters of the magnitude of Job's, but we may experience a tragic accident, become terminally ill, or lose a job and begin asking, "Why me? What does God have against me? Why does God seem so distant?"

During such times, we too often view our circumstances as the enemy and center our prayers on our desire for God to change them. Although Job certainly wanted his miserable circumstances to improve, he also looked beyond those circumstances to his relationship with God. Let's break into groups of three to five and take a closer look to see if Job reveals a different way we can respond to God in the face of our trials.

1. When everything seemed to be stacked against him, what choice did Job's wife urge him to make, and what was his short-term and long-term response? (See Job 2:9–10; 13:15.)

2. Despite their silence upon first seeing Job's plight, Job's three friends— and to a lesser extent a young man named Elihu—had a lot to say. They told Job that a just God treats people fairly and rewards those who obey him. So surely, they reasoned, Job's suffering betrayed some serious, unconfessed sin. For much of the book, they accused and argued their position while Job fought to defend the integrity of his relationship with God.

   Even though Job didn't have the view from "behind the curtain" that we have, he certainly rose to the challenge Satan presented. Read the following passages and note the way Job recognized his human sinfulness, defended his integrity, and clung to God.

Scripture Passage	Job's Response
Job 6:21–29	
Job 9:2–20	
Job 19:2–27	
Job 23:2–12	
Job 27:1–8	

Perspective

Job may have given up on God's justice, but he steadfastly refuses to give up on God. At the most unlikely moments of despair, he comes up with brilliant flashes of hope and faith.... Job instinctively believes he is better off casting his lot with God, regardless of how remote or even sadistic God appears at the moment, rather than abandoning all hope.

—Philip Yancey

3. Despite Job's marvelous faith, Philip Yancey has observed that "Job did not take his pain meekly; he cried out in protest to God. His strong remarks scandalized his friends but not God." When we find ourselves in trying circumstances, we may be afraid of somehow insulting God, so we hesitate to express honestly our pain and doubt.

a. We know from the end of the story that God did not consider Job's honesty to be sin, so consider the following passages and note how strongly Job "let God have it."

Scripture Passage	Job's Accusations
Job 7:17–19; 10:20–21	
Job 14:18–22	
Job 16:7–9	

b. How does this type of expression fit with your picture of what a godly person's relationship with God should look like? What would be your hopes or fears if you dared approach God like this?

Perspective

Job faced a crisis of faith, not of suffering. And so do we. All of us at times find ourselves in a Job-like state.... At such times we focus too easily on circumstances—illness, our looks, poverty, bad luck—as the enemy. We pray for God to change those circumstances.... Job teaches, though, that we need faith most at the precise moment when it seems impossible.

—Philip Yancey

Group Discussion

One Person's Choice Makes a Difference

C. S. Lewis said, "There is no neutral ground in the universe: every square inch, every split second, is claimed by God and counterclaimed by Satan." ... Job presents the astounding truth that our choices of faith matter not just to us and our own destiny but, amazingly, to God himself.... How we respond *matters*. By hanging onto the thinnest thread of faith, Job won a crucial victory in God's grand plan to redeem the earth. In his grace, God has given ordinary men and women the dignity of participating in the redemption of the cosmos.

—Philip Yancey

1. Job's story showed Philip Yancey that "a piece of the history of the universe was at stake in Job, and is still at stake in our own responses," so our choices of faith and our prayers of faith matter to God.

   a. In what ways do you agree or disagree with this statement?

   b. In what ways do you find this hard to believe about yourself?

   c. Can you think of other portions of Scripture that indicate this truth?

Perspective

We will never know, in this life, the full significance of our actions here for, as Job demonstrates, much takes place invisible to us. Jesus' cross offers a pattern for that too: what seemed very ordinary, one more dreary feat of colonial "justice" in a Roman outpost, made possible the salvation of the entire world.

—Philip Yancey

2. At the end of the book of Job, God criticized Job for just one thing: his limited point of view.

   a. In what ways is God's criticism of Job true of us as well?

   b. Why is it so tempting to make judgments about God based on incomplete evidence?

Why Suffering?

The Bible gives many examples of suffering that, like Job's, have nothing to do with God's punishment. In all his miracles of healing, Jesus overturned the notion, widespread at the time, that suffering— blindness, lameness, leprosy—comes to people who deserve it. Jesus grieved over many things that happen on this planet, a sure sign that God regrets them far more than we do. . . . The Bible supplies no systematic answers to the "Why?" questions . . . we dare not tread into areas God has sealed off as his domain. Divine providence is a mystery that only God understands, and belongs in what I have called "The Encyclopedia of Theological Ignorance" for a simple reason: no time-bound human, living on a rebellious planet, blind to the realities of the unseen world, has the ability to comprehend such answers—God's reply to Job in a nutshell.

—Philip Yancey

3. The book of Job shows us that God cares deeply about not only how
   we respond to our distress but how we respond to him when we face
   distress.

   a. Did you realize that we bring God great pleasure when we hon-
      estly put our faith in him?

   b. How does it feel to know that God actually takes delight in his
      relationship with you?

Personal Journey: To Begin Now

The story of Job is a drama of cosmic proportions presented through the context of suffering. The theme of suffering is woven into the fabric of the story, but the story of Job isn't actually about undeserved suffering. It is about having faith in God when faith seems impossible. Take some time now by yourself to consider what you have discovered in this session and how it applies to your daily life.

1. Identify your battleground of faith—career failure, floundering marriage, ill health—the area of life that makes faith in God seem impossible at times. In what ways have you based your faith on who God is, and in what ways have you based it on what he provides?

2. The big question of Job's drama isn't *why* we suffer, but *how* we respond to suffering. The "behind the curtain" glimpse of Job's ordeal that the Bible gives us reveals that in God's plan suffering can serve a higher good. Just as God allowed Job's suffering to occur in order to refute Satan's challenge (which called into question the entire human experiment), God continues to use suffering in ways we may not be able to see or understand.

   a. When the facts don't add up and you see the face of unexplained suffering, how do you typically respond to God?

b. If God audibly spoke to you about how you've responded to him during difficult times, what might he say? You might want to keep his evaluation of Job and his friends (Job 42:7–9) in mind.

c. How would you want God's response to be different?

d. If you believe that God can indeed use suffering for your good— and the good of other people—what impact does that belief have on your life?

3. The book of Job affirms that God hears our cries and is in control of this world no matter how bad things may appear to be. God did not answer all of Job's questions, but in God's presence Job's doubts melted away, and that was enough.

a. When Job came face to face with God, Job saw God in a way he never had before. It seemed to be enough that God ruled the universe and loved him. Is that enough for you? What are the implications of your answer?

b. What are your honest feelings about the statement that God cares more about your response to him than he does about your pleasure? Do you think God can "handle" those feelings? How do those feelings affect your relationship with God?

Perspective

When a Job-like circumstance happens to you, I guarantee you that someone has been there before you. And that's the old man Job. Because he was honest, because he was so eloquent, he's like a pioneer. He has gone ahead of us. So if you wonder, *Should I really feel that? Should I really say that to God?* you can relax and say, "Well, yeah, that's okay because Job already did."

—Philip Yancey

Personal Journey: To Do between Sessions

Before the next session, set aside time away from distractions to ask God to draw you closer to him.

1. Seek to deepen your relationship with God so that you can respond in faith when you face challenges that make faith seem impossible. The passages below will help remind you of God's care for those who turn to him in their distress. Read and meditate on each one and write a short journal entry focusing on how deeply God cares for his suffering servants.

Scripture Passage	God's Care for Those Who Trust Him
Psalm 9:9–10	
Psalm 33:12–19	
Psalm 34:15–22	
Isaiah 46:9–11	
Isaiah 49:13–16	
Nahum 1:7	

2. Some of God's most righteous and faithful people have had to endure great trials. In Ezekiel 14:14, God mentions Job, Daniel, and Noah. We have focused on Job's story in this session, but you may also want to read about Daniel's trial (Daniel 6) and Noah's trial (Genesis 6:5–22; 7:13–18; 8).

Deuteronomy: A Taste of Bittersweet

Like a parent trying to teach an unruly bunch of children how to behave as adults ... Moses had one last shot, one last opportunity to pass along historical memory, to purge himself of grievances and pain, to bequeath to them the hope and grit they would desperately need in his absence.

—Philip Yancey

Questions to Think About

1. What do you know about the book of Deuteronomy? What do you think God's purpose was in preserving its message for us?

2. Would you say you are more attentive and obedient to God when things in your life are going well or when you are facing difficulties? Explain your answer and share some examples from your life.

3. Most of us would say that we remember the basics of our faith. We would claim to remember the important stories in Scripture and to remember what God teaches us. But how well do we *really* remember what God says? Let's take a few moments to name as many of the Ten Commandments as we can.

Video Presentation: "Deuteronomy: A Taste of Bittersweet"

A perspective on history

Moses speaks
Things are looking up. Don't blow it!

Remember where you came from

God chooses a people to create a culture

Deuteronomy for our time

Video Highlights

1. At the beginning, Philip said, "When things are really going well, that's when you are in danger. Look out. Watch out." Explain why it's easier to forget about God when things are going well. What biblical or contemporary examples of this principle come to mind?

2. Moses had spent more than a generation leading the Hebrews to the Promised Land. He had known them when they suffered as slaves in Egypt. For more than forty years he had seen them at their best and at their worst. He had listened, coaxed, scolded, fasted, taught, suffered, prayed, judged, mediated, and so much more—all on their behalf.

   a. What do you think Moses must have felt as he stood before that vast throng and prepared to speak to them for the last time?

   b. Why do you think Moses thought it was so important to teach the Hebrews' history to this new generation? If you had been Moses, what do you think you would have been compelled to tell them before you died?

Did You Know?

Nothing, apparently, bothers God more than the simple act of being forgotten. . . . On the first day they [the Israelites] ate produce from the Promised Land, the manna would stop. From then on they must cultivate their own land and plant their own crops. They would build cities, fight wars, appoint a king. They would prosper and grow plump. They would trust their armies and chariots instead of their God, forgetting the lesson inflicted on almighty Egypt. They would discriminate against the poor and the aliens, forgetting they were once both. In a word, they would forget God.

—Philip Yancey

Large Group Exploration: Get Ready ... Get Set ... Remember!

In the video, Philip Yancey said, "Moses was saying, 'You are ready now. Don't blow it. . . . This is a new generation. It's a new world, and I want you to go into this land with hope and promise and confidence that your parents who had started off as slaves in Egypt never felt.'"

Moses took definite steps to encourage the people to focus their minds and hearts on God as they entered the Promised Land. Let's look at some of those steps and consider how they apply to our lives today.

1. God had specific requirements for his people to obey so that they could reap all of the blessings of the land he had promised. What did Moses tell the people to do in order to impress upon them the importance of their obedience? (See Deuteronomy 6:1–9; 11:18–21.)

2. Which annual celebration did Moses establish, and why? (See Deuteronomy 16:1–8.)

3. What did Moses and the elders command the people to do as soon as they crossed the Jordan River and entered the Promised Land? Why do you think they commanded this? (See Deuteronomy 27:1–8.)

4. Even though Moses had already commanded the people to remember and obey God in the activities of daily life, through a celebratory feast and by the building of monuments, he provided additional reminders.

   a. What else did Moses command the people to do, and why? (See Deuteronomy 27:11–26.)

   b. What other musical memorial did God command Moses to write? What was its purpose? (See Deuteronomy 31:19–22.)

Perspective

During the years of wilderness wanderings, forced to depend on God daily, the Hebrews did not have the luxury of forgetting. God fed the Israelites, clothed them, planned their daily itinerary, and fought their battles. No Hebrew questioned the existence of God in those days, for he hovered before them in a thick cloud and a pillar of fire.

—Philip Yancey

5. Deuteronomy 8 could be viewed as a representative summary of the book of Deuteronomy. What is the recurring theme of this chapter?

Deuteronomy 8	Theme
vv. 1–2	
vv. 10–14	
vv. 17–18	
vv. 19–20	

Remember to Remember

God wanted his people to remember their history so that they would not forget to obey him. The verses below highlight just a few of the truths and events God wanted his people to remember. Consider each truth or event and the impact that memory could have on one's relationship with God.

Verses in Deuteronomy	What the Israelites Were to Remember
4:10–12	The day they stood before the Lord at Horeb and heard his words from the fire
5:15	How God miraculously removed them from slavery in Egypt
7:18–19	What God did to Pharaoh and all Egypt
8:2–4	How God had led them and cared for them in the desert for forty years
8:18	The God who gave them the ability to produce wealth and so confirmed his covenant with them
9:7–14	How their repeated sin so provoked God that he wanted to destroy them
24:17–22	That they were once slaves in Egypt, so they were to care for the alien, the fatherless, and the widowed

---

Small Group Exploration: A Peculiar People

During the video presentation, Philip spoke about God calling the Hebrews "my peculiar people." They were to be different from any other nation. They were to think differently. They were to act differently. They were, in a nutshell, to be God's *holy* people, God's "set apart" people who would show others what God is like. Let's break into groups of three to five and take a look at a few passages in Deuteronomy that will help us understand what God had in mind for the people who would represent him to the world.

1. What was unique about the Hebrews? (See Deuteronomy 7:6–9.)

2. In Deuteronomy 7:12–14, we see how serious God considers his covenant to be. What did the Hebrews have to do in order to receive the benefits of God's covenant with them?

3. After Moses reviewed all the terms of God's covenant to the people, note what Moses emphasized. (See Deuteronomy 26:16–19.)

   a. What were the people to do (v. 16)?

b. What did Moses remind the people that they had declared (v. 17)?

c. What did Moses say God had declared (vv. 18–19)?

Did You Know?

Success, not failure, is the greatest danger facing any follower of God, as Moses knew well. . . . Every significant downfall in his own life came when he seized power for himself—killing an Egyptian, smashing a rock in the desert—rather than relying on God.

—Philip Yancey

4. We've seen how Moses emphasized the importance of the Hebrews knowing God's laws, applying those laws in daily life, and teaching those laws to their children. As Christians today, we, too, are to represent God to the world around us. To what extent do you think God's laws impact (or ought to impact) the way we live? How might our relationships with God and with other people change if we truly made obedience to God our overarching priority in daily life?

Group Discussion

1. Deuteronomy is essentially a record of the Hebrew people's oral history. In what ways does an oral history differ from what we might read in a textbook?

2a. As modern people, we learn about history from textbooks. In what ways do we also create highlights or reviews of our history that function a bit like an oral history?

b. What do these memorials of and monuments to our history do for us? In what ways do they change or influence our behavior?

Perspective

With the speeches in Deuteronomy, Moses established the great tradition of historical memory, a tradition his people, who became known as the Jews, have cherished ever since: "Never forget." Try as we might, we can never undo the past, but still we must honor it by bearing witness, by remembering so as not to allow it to repeat.
—Philip Yancey

3. What would you say is the most important thing for us to remember from this session?

Independence Day

The United States celebrates July 4 like no other day. The parades, the picnics, and the fireworks boisterously express national pride. We showed 'em, say the politicians in their speeches. With our own sweat and blood we created a nation. We're proud to be Americans.

Our style of celebration—noisy and flag-waving and proud—captures something of the original spirit that led a young nation to declare independence. A similar spirit surges up in France on Bastille Day and in many other nations on their birthdays. But these celebrations bear a striking *unlikeness* to the Jewish independence day, a day called Passover.

The Jews trace their cultural birthday back to a dark, foreboding night—the Israelites' last in Egypt (Exodus 12). There are no blaring bands nor balloons nor fireworks to commemorate this event. Everything takes place inside a home, with a family or cluster of families gathered around a table. Participants taste morsels of food, pausing before each portion to hear Old Testament accounts of the history they are reliving. Their independence day resembles a worship service, not a party.

More than anything else, the Jewish independence day expresses this one fact: God did it. No Israelite armies stood against the mighty Egyptians. Freedom came in the blackest night while Israelite families huddled around the Passover table, their bags packed, waiting for deliverance.

—*The Student Bible*, 95

Personal Journey: To Begin Now

Deuteronomy records Moses' parting words as the Hebrews stood ready to cross the Jordan River and possess the Promised Land. Success—the land of milk and honey—was at last within their grasp, and Moses saw trouble ahead. He had learned that success is dangerous, so in the strongest terms he warned them to be careful.

Take some time now by yourself to reflect quietly on your walk with God and consider what God would have you do to remember what he has done for you in the past.

1. When we are in trouble, we may find it easy to turn to God—for help, guidance, strength, and hope. But we often pay less attention to God, or ignore him altogether, when things are going well for us.

   a. What typically happens in your relationship with God when life is difficult?

   b. When life becomes more comfortable?

2a. If Moses knew you as well as he knew the Hebrews, what might be his concerns regarding your commitment to walk with God?

   b. What might Moses' parting words be to you?

Personal Journey: To Do between Sessions

Over and over again, Moses commanded the people not to forget about God. The tired old man who talked with God challenged them to remember what God had done for them. He reminded them that God had chosen them to be his holy people. He urged them to remember where they had been so they could go where they were destined to go.

1. God wants a personal relationship with us. He wants us not to forget what he has done for us in the past, what he is doing for us today, and what he will do for us tomorrow. What comes between you and God that keeps you from remembering and acting on the presence of God in your life?

Perspective

Life with God is never so easy, so settled, for any of us. Not for the Hebrews then, and not for us living today. The pilgrim must ever progress, uphill, meeting new enemies around every bend.

—Philip Yancey

2. Moses and the elders established a variety of activities to help keep God and his laws foremost in the minds of his people (Deuteronomy 16, 27). Which activities would help focus your heart and mind toward God and on what it means to obey him? Which of those activities, or spiritual disciplines, do you presently practice? Which of those activities might you want to add to your life?

3. If you were to erect "standing stones" to commemorate God's faithfulness to you, how many different piles would you have to build? What would each of them commemorate?

God's Personal Nature

During his experience with God and the Israelites, Moses rediscovered a fundamental fact about God: He is a person. Whereas the Egyptians and Canaanites viewed their gods as distant, unapproachable, capricious, and unpredictable, the Israelites grew to understand that their God was quite different. Their God:

- Was as personal as they themselves
- Spoke to them and listened to them
- Felt pain and jealousy when his people were unfaithful
- Negotiated and signed contracts
- Expressed his love for humanity
- Insisted on holiness but was also willing to forgive
- Established boundaries for behavior that could be understood and obeyed
- Gave out mercy as well as discipline
- Desired honor
- Longed for his covenant with the Hebrews to succeed
- Met with Moses face to face

Psalms: Spirituality in Every Key

Poetry works its magic subtly. . . . We turn to it because the poet's shaping of words and images gives us pleasure and moves our emotions. Yet if the poet succeeds, we may gain something greater than knowledge: a transformed vision. That is the magic the psalms have ultimately worked upon me. They have transformed my spiritual vision and my understanding of relationship with God.

—Philip Yancey

Questions to Think About

1. What has been your experience in reading the psalms, and what do you expect to find when you read them?

2. How do your perceptions of and feelings toward the psalms change when you read just a few of them in contrast to when you try to read a number of them straight through?

3. Would you dare to say to God some of the things the psalmists have said? Why or why not?

Video Presentation: "The Psalms: Spirituality in Every Key"

The psalms:
  Prayers about life with God

Timeless poetry from a "golden age"

Deeply honest expression before God

Reading the psalms

Video Highlights

1. Philip Yancey said he sometimes finds it hard to express his deepest feelings to God and that the book of Psalms has become a guidebook for him, helping him to express in words what he is feeling. What do you think about this idea? Why?

2. What do you think would be the benefit of Philip Yancey's suggestion that we search the psalms until we find one that reflects where we are at a given moment—and then meditate on that particular psalm?

3. The following chart gives a few references to the psalms from the book of Matthew. How does it affect your appreciation of the psalms to realize that God's people have read, memorized, sung, discussed, and pondered these expressive prayers to God for thousands of years?

What is your response when you realize that the words of a psalm that expresses what you are thinking or feeling today were penned about 3,000 years ago?

Did You Know?

The New Testament books include many references to the book of Psalms. Some of these references occur in conversations Jesus had with other people, while other references were chosen by various New Testament authors to make a point. It is obvious from these New Testament references that phrases and ideas from the psalms were well known and commonly used by the general public of Jesus' day. The following list highlights just a few such references found in the book of Matthew.

New Testament Link to a Psalm	Psalm Source
Matthew 4:6—Satan quoted from Psalm 91 when he tempted Jesus	Psalm 91:11–12
Matthew 13:35—Matthew recognized that Jesus' words were a fulfillment of the prophecy: "I will open my mouth in parables, I will utter things hidden . . . ."	Psalm 78:2
Matthew 21:42—Jesus quoted from Psalm 118 when asking a key question	Psalm 118:22–23
Matthew 22:44—Jesus used the first verse of Psalm 110 to confound some Pharisees	Psalm 110:1
Matthew 23:39—Jesus reveals his extensive knowledge of the psalms	Psalm 118:26
Matthew 27:46—Matthew recorded Jesus' words, realizing that they fulfilled a prophecy from Psalm 22	Psalm 22:1

Large Group Exploration: Understanding an Anthology of Personal Letters

Philip Yancey writes, "For the Hebrew poets, God represented a reality more solid than their own whipsaw emotions or the checkered history of their people. They wrestled with God over every facet of their lives, and in the end it was the very act of wrestling that proved their faith." One way to approach the book of Psalms is to think of it as a collection of personal letters that, when put together, reveals a panoramic picture of humanity wrestling with God. Let's consider the perspective these letters provide.

1. In what ways does approaching the book of Psalms as an anthology of poetry change your expectations for this book?

2. Part of what the psalms give us is a unique look into David's soul—the soul of a man who loved God. Various psalms reveal his delight, his frustration, and the ways in which he reconciled the events of his life with what he knew of God. Let's take a quick look at some circumstances of David's life and the psalms he wrote during those times.

Circumstances of David's Life: His Outward Journey	The Psalms David Wrote: His Inward Journey
1 Samuel 21:10–15: David feigns madness in a successful attempt to keep from being killed by the Philistines.	Psalm 56:
1 Samuel 19:1–17: David sneaks out of a window while his wife diverts pursuers sent by King Saul to kill him.	Psalm 59:
1 and 2 Samuel: David is chased around by his enemies for years and has to fight all-night battles.	Psalm 18:
2 Samuel 12:1–14: Nathan confronted David concerning his sin with Bathsheba and his murder of her husband, Uriah.	Psalm 51:

a. As you compare each psalm to the circumstance in which David wrote it, what relationship do you see between the psalm and the situation in which it was written? Do you find what you expected?

b. What do you discover from these psalms about David's view of God's work in his life?

c. What did David express that reveals his confidence that he mattered to God? (See Psalm 18:19.)

Perspective

In my fixation with the details of the psalms . . . I had missed the main point, which is that the book of Psalms comprises a sampling of spiritual journals, much like personal letters to God. . . . They are personal prayers in the form of poetry, written by a variety of people—peasants, kings, professional musicians, rank amateurs—in wildly fluctuating moods. . . . examples of "ordinary" people struggling mightily to align what they believe about God with what they actually experience.

—Philip Yancey

Small Group Exploration: A Guidebook for Sharing Our Hearts with God

God wants us to express our deepest feelings to him, not to pretend to be something we are not. "Doubt, paranoia, giddiness, meanness, delight, hatred, joy, praise, vengefulness, betrayal—you can find it all in Psalms," Philip Yancey writes. "Such strewing of emotions, which I once saw as hopeless disarray, I now see as a sign of health. From Psalms I have learned that I can rightfully bring to God whatever I feel about him. I need not paper over my failures and try to clean up my own rottenness; far better to bring those weaknesses to God, who alone has the power to heal."

Let's break into groups of three to five and look more closely at the emotions expressed in a few psalms.

1. Poetry is an expression of the soul—the thoughts and feelings that resonate deep within our hearts. Let's look at a sampling of passages from the book of Psalms and note the range and depth of emotion the psalmists express to God.

   a. Psalm 13:1–4

   b. Psalm 30:11–12

   c. Psalm 34:4–22

d. Psalm 38:1–15

e. Psalm 42

f. Psalm 58

2. In what way(s) have you been encouraged to express or discouraged from expressing what you really think and feel to God? How might understanding the book of Psalms as a collection of heartfelt poems or letters written to God encourage you to share more honestly with God?

Perspective

More than any other book in the Bible, Psalms reveals what a heart-felt, soul-starved, single-minded relationship with God looks like.

—Philip Yancey

Group Discussion

1. The book of Psalms comprises a remarkable anthology of literature that has had an impact on the Jewish and Christian faiths for more than 3,000 years! As we've seen, the psalms do not exist primarily to tell a story or teach principles of doctrine; they are, instead, a collection of personal letters to God that show us what relationship with God looks like. In a deeply personal way, they help us reconcile what we believe about life with what we actually encounter in life. Why is it important for us to reorient our daily experiences to the spiritual world—to the reality of God and our relationship with him?

2. The 150 psalms cover the entire spectrum of our relationship with God—the happy times, times of praise, the sad times, times of woundedness, and times of confusion. As such, these prayers in poetry can help us honestly express our feelings to God, including feelings we may find difficult to express such as rage, doubt, paranoia, meanness, delight, joy, praise, and betrayal. In what ways might we benefit from using the psalms to bring our deepest feelings to God?

Personal Journey: To Begin Now

Even if it is little more than a vague memory of Psalm 23, nearly all of us have some exposure to the book of Psalms. Take some time now by yourself to quietly consider what else the psalms might offer you as you grow in your walk with God.

1. At one point in his efforts to understand the book of Psalms, Philip Yancey wrote, "People around me used the book as a spiritual medicine cabinet ... an approach that never worked for me. With uncanny consistency I would land on a psalm that aggravated, rather than cured, my problem. Martin Marty judges at least half the psalms to be 'wintry' in tone, and when feeling low I would accidentally turn to one of the wintriest and end up frostily depressed."

   a. How would you describe your personal experience with the psalms thus far?

   b. If your experience with the psalms has been less than satisfying to you, what have you learned during this session that may help you experience the psalms in a new way?

2. Much of this session has focused on the importance of expressing the depth of our thoughts and feelings about life to God.

    a. In what ways has this session encouraged you to be more honest and open in your relationship with God?

    b. What makes it difficult for you to really level with God about your deepest pain, struggles, and insecurities?

    c. What do you want to do about these obstacles?

Personal Journey: To Do between Sessions

Many of us feel overwhelmed at the prospect of actually writing a psalm, but if we view it as a process of focusing on God and honestly expressing our thoughts, questions, and feelings about how our lives relate to him, it might not be so hard after all. The steps listed below will help guide you through the process of writing a psalm to God about your life and relationship with him.

1. *What significant things—events, people, places, thoughts—are happening in my life?* Look at a portion of your life. It could be what happened today, during the past week, or even a short segment of any time in your life. It could be a situation that inspired great joy or great sorrow. Write out several short phrases or one-word descriptions of what happened, your thoughts, your feelings, which objects or events were involved, your questions for God:

   Object or event:

   My feelings:

   What I think/thought:

   Questions for God:

2. *What can I express to God?* Sometimes we hesitate to really express to God what we are feeling. We either don't seem to have the right words to say or we're afraid to say them. But chances are, whether we want to praise God or tell him our woes, one or more psalms has already expressed a similar thought. By reading a few psalms, you may become more comfortable with the idea of expressing yourself to God.

   a. Praises—read Psalm 8:1–9; 66:1–7; 98:4–9
   b. Laments—read Psalm 94:1–10; 102:1–11; 123

3. *Take it to God!* Using the words you wrote above as a framework, write a psalm to God. If you are uncomfortable writing a psalm, perhaps one of the psalms you read above (or another one you find) already provides the words that express what you want to say to God. If so, meditate on that psalm. Read it, sing it, or memorize it over a period of days. As you write and meditate on the psalm, ask God to reveal himself to you and to continue to teach you more about himself and your relationship with him.

Ecclesiastes: The End of Wisdom

The same lesson Job learned in dust and ashes—that we humans cannot figure out life on our own—the Teacher learns in a robe and palace. In the end, the Teacher freely admits that life does not make sense outside of God and will never fully make sense because we are not God. . . . Unless we acknowledge our limits and subject ourselves to God's rule, unless we trust the Giver of all good gifts, we will end up in a state of despair. Ecclesiastes calls us to accept our status as creatures under the dominion of the Creator, something few of us do without a struggle.

—Philip Yancey

Questions to Think About

1. When someone mentions the book of Ecclesiastes, what words immediately come to mind? Why?

2. The Bible says that every person needs God, yet some people don't seem to need God at all. They live rich, apparently fulfilling lives without giving God a single thought. In fact, they seem to be doing quite well without him. How can this be?

3. Some people living in the affluent cultures of the West have every
   material thing they need and much of what they want, yet are so overwhelmed by despair they don't know why they should go on living.
   Some of them even end their own lives. What do you think leads
   prosperous people to despair?

Video Presentation: "Ecclesiastes: The End of Wisdom"

What do you make of Ecclesiastes?

Roots of despair

God goes where he is wanted, to people who know they need him

"Papering over" our need for God during the good times

A time for everything

Video Highlights

1. If we believe that all Scripture is inspired by God, we have to conclude that God wanted Ecclesiastes—a book that focuses on meaninglessness—to be in the Bible. What might be the reasons God wanted the message of Ecclesiastes to be a part of the Bible?

2. Does the theme, "Be careful that you don't forget about God when you grow prosperous and things are going well," sound familiar? Where have you heard it before, and why might we need to hear it again?

3. In what ways do you agree or disagree with the statement that "times of prosperity are dangerous because we then find it easier to ignore God"? What personal experience can you contribute to our discussion?

4. Jesus added a whole new dimension to the meaning of life when he said we gain the world by giving our lives away in service to others, not by accumulating as much as we can. How does this fit with your experience?

Perspective

Ecclesiastes sounded its note of doom in an era of unprecedented prosperity and social progress. The ruler over Israel could sense within himself and his nation the failure to sustain the burden. He learned the hard lesson Moses had tried to teach the Israelites centuries before: whatever humans touch will bear a fatal flaw. Good times represent the real danger; our best efforts spell ruin. In short, human beings are not gods, and that realization drove the Teacher to despair.

—Philip Yancey

Large Group Exploration: Despair in an Age of Prosperity?

The "good life" enjoyed by so many people who live in affluent Western cultures is riddled with despair. Many people are trapped in the belief that life is meaningless, yet they hotly pursue the illusions of meaning anyway! This is the same trap that caught the anonymous Teacher of Ecclesiastes. Let's see what he discovered about life and despair.

1. Despite all the pleasures he tasted and all the things he pursued and accomplished in order to find meaning and purpose, the Teacher in Ecclesiastes found that nothing the world offered added a shred of meaning to his life. Let's look up the following verses and discuss his pursuits and perspective.

What the Teacher Pursued	What the Teacher Discovered
Ecclesiastes 1:13, 16–17:	Ecclesiastes 1:18; 2:16:
Ecclesiastes 2:1–3:	Ecclesiastes 6:7–9; 7:2, 4–6:
Ecclesiastes 2:4–6:	Ecclesiastes 2:17–18:
Ecclesiastes 2:8:	Ecclesiastes 2:21; 5:10–12:
Ecclesiastes 2:9:	Ecclesiastes 3:19–20:

Perspective

A despairing book like Ecclesiastes will more likely emerge from a Golden Age. Consider the contrast between Ecclesiastes and Job. They cover many of the same themes—life's unfairness, why suffering exists, why evil people prosper and good ones suffer—but what a difference in tone! Ecclesiastes exudes meaninglessness and futility while Job rings with betrayal, passion, and a cry for justice. Job shakes his fist at God, calls him into account, demands a reply. The Teacher shrugs his shoulders, mumbles, "So what?" and reaches for another goblet of wine.... The tone of Ecclesiastes captures precisely the mood of affluent Western countries.

—Philip Yancey

2. Many of us who live in affluent Western cultures find ourselves walking down a path similar to that of the Teacher of Ecclesiastes. The late Bruno Bettelheim observed, "We should be living in a dawn of great promise. But now that we are freer to enjoy life, we are deeply frustrated in our disappointment that the freedom and comfort, sought with such deep desire, do not give meaning and purpose to our lives." Meaninglessness plagues us just as it did the Teacher. What about life leads us to these feelings of meaninglessness and despair?

3. One of the fascinating aspects of Ecclesiastes is that the Teacher presents his views on the meaninglessness of life in juxtaposition to the

reality of God. Surprisingly, his conclusion offers the antidote to despair. What is his conclusion, and what is its relevance to us? (See Ecclesiastes 12:9–14.)

Did You Know?

Although the Teacher of Ecclesiastes eventually concluded that the whole duty of humankind is to fear God and keep his command-ments, much of the book views daily life from a purely human per-spective. In contrast, the writer of Proverbs offers practical wisdom for daily living that is focused more on God. Note the contrasts in the following passages.

Ecclesiastes on Daily Life	Proverbs on Daily Life
I devoted myself to study and to explore by wisdom all that is done under heaven. What a heavy bur-den God has laid on men! . . . For with much wisdom comes much sorrow; the more knowledge, the more grief (1:13,18).	The LORD gives wisdom, and from his mouth come knowledge and understanding (2:6).
The wise man has eyes in his head, while the fool walks in darkness; but I came to realize that the same fate overtakes them both. . . . What then do I gain by being wise? (2:14, 15).	Trust in the LORD with all your heart and lean not on your own understanding (3:5).
. . . The abundance of a rich man permits him no sleep (5:12).	The blessing of the LORD brings wealth, and he adds no trouble to it (10:22).
A feast is made for laughter, and wine makes life merry, but money is the answer for everything (10:19).	Whoever trusts in his riches will fall, but the righteous will thrive like a green leaf (11:28).

Small Group Exploration: A Tale of Two Kingdoms

Hovering in the background of Ecclesiastes is the truth that meaningful human life involves more than the visible world we see. Philip Yancey describes the book as presenting "both sides of life on this planet: the promise of pleasures so alluring that we may devote our lives to their pursuit, and then the haunting realization that these pleasures ultimately do not satisfy."

He goes on to explain why the visible world—what we can call the visible kingdom—is not enough: "God's tantalizing world is too big for us. Made for another home, made for eternity, we finally realize that nothing this side of timeless Paradise will quiet the rumors of discontent." So as much as we crave the visible kingdom, our hearts seem to know that we were created to belong in another.

Let's break into groups of three to five and take a few moments to highlight the life and kingdom of King Solomon—the shadow figure of Ecclesiastes—and contrast it with the invisible kingdom of another King.

1. What was the status of the visible kingdom of Israel during Solomon's reign? What illustrates its peace and prosperity? (See 1 Kings 4:25, 34; 10:1–5, 23.)

2. What happened to Solomon as time passed? (See 1 Kings 11:1–10.)

3. What happened to his kingdom after Solomon's death? (See 1 Kings 12:1–7, 16–17, 26–30.)

4. Many years later, Jesus came to establish a much different kingdom. Where is this kingdom? (See John 18:36.)

Did You Know?

Jesus' perspective on "the good life" differs radically from that of the Teacher of Ecclesiastes. Jesus expressed his perspective to his disciples when he said:

Blessed are you who are poor, for yours is the kingdom of God. Blessed are you who hunger now, for you will be satisfied. Blessed are you who weep now, for you will laugh. Blessed are you when men hate you, when they exclude you and insult you and reject your name as evil, because of the Son of Man. Rejoice in that day and leap for joy, because great is your reward in heaven. For that is how their fathers treated the prophets. But woe to you who are rich, for you have already received your comfort. Woe to you who are well fed now, for you will go hungry. Woe to you who laugh now, for you will mourn and weep. Woe to you when all men speak well of you, for that is how their fathers treated the false prophets (Luke 6:20–26).

5. What did Jesus reveal about the visible and invisible kingdoms in his parable of the rich fool and in his conversations with the Pharisees? (See Luke 12:16–21; 16:13–15.)

6. How is what Jesus said to his disciples similar to what the Teacher in Ecclesiastes said at the end of his book? (See Matthew 16:24–27; Ecclesiastes 12:13–14.)

Perspective

The account of decadence by the richest, wisest, most talented person in the world serves as a perfect allegory for what can happen when we lose sight of the Giver whose good gifts we enjoy. Pleasure represents a great good but also a grave danger. If we start chasing pleasure as an end in itself, along the way we may lose sight of the One who gave us such good gifts as sexual drive, taste buds, and the capacity to appreciate beauty. In that event, as Ecclesiastes tells it, a wholesale devotion to pleasure will paradoxically lead to a state of utter despair.

—Philip Yancey

Group Discussion

1. In what ways have your opinions of Ecclesiastes changed as a result of this session?

2. Philip Yancey quotes J. I. Packer as calling Ecclesiastes the "one book in Scripture that is expressly designed to turn us into realists." Why do you think he came to this conclusion, and in what ways do you agree or disagree with it?

3. Name some people—personal acquaintances, Bible characters, notable people from history, or well-known contemporary people— who seem to have found peace and meaning in life. What do you think gives them peace and meaning?

Personal Journey: To Begin Now

Ecclesiastes portrays the inevitable consequences when God is not at the center of human life. Written from the perspective of the Teacher, who has tried it all and done so in excess, the existential tone of the book matches the despair of our affluent Western culture. Take some time now by yourself to consider what you have discovered in this session and how it applies to your life.

1. In the end, the Teacher freely admits that life doesn't (and can never) make sense apart from God. Describe an experience that might have led you to the realization that life doesn't make sense or is unfair.

   a. What was your emotional response to that realization?

   b. If you were to honestly share your thoughts and feelings about the meaning of life with God and heard his answer, how do you think your perspective might change?

2. Ecclesiastes conveys to all of humankind the same message Moses conveyed to the Hebrews in Deuteronomy: Fear God and keep his commandments. It's a tough message for people who have it all. We must be ever cautious that we don't "paper over" our need for God, because the greatest danger we face as humans is to have what we need and forget about him.

   a. In what ways are you tempted to create your own little "kingdom"—having pride in what you have done and plan to do—apart from God?

   b. If you were to take to heart the Teacher's advice, "Fear God and keep his commandments," what difference do you think it would make in your life? In the lives of people around you?

Personal Journey: To Do between Sessions

As a result of his study, Philip Yancey writes, "I have come to see Ecclesiastes not as a mistake, nor as a contrived form of reverse apologetics, rather as a profound reminder of the limits of being human. Ecclesiastes sets forth the inevitable consequences of a life without God at the center, and the pitfalls it warns against endanger the believer as much as the pagan."

1. What limits of being human do you have a hard time facing?

2. In what ways are you depending on the visible world to "paper over" your human limits?

3. In what ways are you trying to find meaning in what this world has to offer?

4. What are the pitfalls and consequences of living without God in those areas of your life?

5. Take some time this week to read and meditate on Chapters 2 and 3 of Ecclesiastes, particularly verses 2:10–11; 17–26; 3:9–15. Note the difference in perspective between living in light of the visible world only as opposed to living in light of God's perspective. Ask God to reveal to you the ways you are searching for meaning apart from him.

The Prophets: God Talks Back

Why read the prophets? There is one compelling reason: to get to know God. The prophets are the Bible's most forceful revelation of God's personality.... One who reads the prophets encounters not an impassible, distant deity but an actual Person, a God as passionate as any person you have met. God feels delight, and frustration, and anger. He weeps and moans with pain.... The prophets proclaim loud and clear how God feels: he loves us.

—Philip Yancey

Questions to Think About

1. When you think of the prophetic books of the Bible such as Amos, Obadiah, Jeremiah, Daniel, Isaiah, and Habakkuk, which words, images, and feelings come to mind?

2. From what you know of the Bible, what do you think God is like? In what ways does your understanding of God as portrayed in the prophets differ from your understanding of him as presented elsewhere in Scripture?

3. What did the Old Testament prophets actually do?

4. If you knew that something terrible was going to happen to every-
   body within twenty miles of your home a week from today unless
   everyone repented of their sin and turned to God, what would you
   do? How far would you go to tell your message? What might people
   think of you for doing it?

Video Presentation: "The Prophets: God Talks Back"

God talks back: his personality revealed

Understanding the prophets

Crazy guys doing whatever it takes to make the point

Prophets in context

Making the prophets personal

Video Highlights

1. One of the things that helped open up the books of the prophets for Philip Yancey was to view them more as a revelation of God's personality than a revelation of history or the future. In what ways might that change in approach affect our ability to appreciate these books?

2. When you consider the lengths to which the prophets went in order to communicate God's message, what would have been your response if God had chosen you to be a prophet and given you an important message to communicate to your society?

3. Describe a time in your reading of the prophets when you have experienced a point of strong identity with a prophet, particularly his feelings or perceptions. What about a time when certain words "jumped off the page" and touched a deep need in your heart?

Did You Know?

I found the prophets to be the most "modern" writers imaginable. In chapter after chapter they deal with the very same themes that hang like a cloud over our century: the silence of God, economic disparity, injustice, war, the seeming sovereignty of evil, the unrelieved suffering that afflicts our world. These, the same themes that surface periodically in Job, Psalms, Ecclesiastes, and even Deuteronomy, the prophets bring into sharp focus, as if examining them under a microscope.

—Philip Yancey

Large Group Exploration: Getting to Know the God Who Loves Us

The prophets, although they may seem terribly foreign and distant to us, reveal amazingly intimate exchanges between God and his people. Faced with people who weren't listening to God, the prophets experienced the anguish of seeing God seemingly pulling farther and farther away from his creation. They challenged him to miraculously display his power as he did in the days of Moses. They asked him tough questions: "Why is there so much poverty?" "Why don't you *speak* and *act* now?" In response to their questions, God answered! He revealed his innermost thoughts—his passion, his delight, his anger, and his frustration. Most important, he revealed how very much we matter to him.

Let's consider a few passages from the prophets that will help us become better acquainted with the God who loves us.

1. The prophets expressed themselves honestly—sometimes brutally so—to God. Let's see just how strongly they expressed themselves. (See Isaiah 64:7, 10–12; Jeremiah 14:8–9; Habakkuk 1:2–4.)

2. Sometimes God responds in anger when we show disregard for him. At other times he responds more like a wounded lover, weeping and moaning with pain. Let's look at a sampling of his responses in the books of the prophets. What do we learn about God through them?

Scripture	God's Response
Habakkuk 1:2–7	
Isaiah 51:4, 11	
Jeremiah 3:12–15	
Zephaniah 3:17	
Hosea 11:8–10	

3. The prophets reveal how very much God's people matter to him. Read Jeremiah 31:3–14. What evidence do we find in this passage that we matter to God?

Did You Know?

One important message shines through with great force: God passionately desires his people. Above all else, the prophets repeat the constant refrain of the Old Testament, that we *matter* to God.

—Philip Yancey

Small Group Exploration: A Fresh Look at the Prophets

We're going to do something a bit different in our small groups today. After breaking into groups of three to five, have someone in your group read the Scripture passage listed. Then discuss the questions that follow, using the perspectives we have gained from this session to make these intimidating books more approachable.

Read Micah 4:1–5:2.

1. In *The Bible Jesus Read,* Philip Yancey provides some tips for reading the prophets. He categorizes the prophet's insights roughly into three categories, which will help you overcome barriers you may have against reading the prophets, and also help you to discover the books' essential messages: (1) *Now prophecies* relate primarily to situations in each prophet's own day; (2) *Later prophecies* are well removed from each prophet's own time but were later fulfilled in history; and (3) *Much later prophecies* seem still to lie in the future.

    Which *now, later,* or *much later* prophecies can you identify in Micah 4:1–5:2?

2. "As 'seers,' the prophets have insight into God's perspective," Philip Yancey explains. "Keep in mind that the prophets didn't tell us when the predicted events will happen and sometimes combine near and distant predictions in the same paragraph. . . . Sequence is a minor issue for the God who lives outside the constraints of time."

   What from this passage indicates that sequence was a minor issue for the prophet?

3. Sometimes the books of the prophets permit us to glimpse into the cosmic view of history—the history behind the history. In Daniel 10, for example, an angel explained to Daniel that "the prince of the Persian kingdom" had prevented him from answering Daniel's prayer for twenty-one days. Finally, reinforcements arrived, and Michael— a chief angel—helped him break through the opposition. So Daniel played a decisive role in the warfare between cosmic forces of good and evil, though much of the action was beyond his range of vision.

   Which portions of this passage are indicative of God's cosmic view—a view that we have a hard time grasping?

4. In what ways do you see God's personality—his thoughts, feelings, character—revealed through this passage?

5. Philip Yancey notes that "the prophets call us beyond the fears and grim reality of present history to the view of all eternity, to a time when God's reign will fill the earth with light and truth."

   Which portion(s) of this passage give you a glimpse of God's ultimate viewpoint and give you hope to endure the challenges of your life?

Perspective

The prophets ... render God's point of view. God granted them (and, through them, us) the extraordinary vision to see past this world, dominated as it is by great powers and larger-than-life tyrants, to a different level of reality. We get a glimpse, a mere glimpse, of history from God's viewpoint. No wonder the prophets seem strange: we lack the capacity for seeing the world from the vantage point of timelessness.

—Philip Yancey

Group Discussion

1. Would one or two of you please share some highlights of your small group discussion with the whole group?

2. The following portion of *The Bible Jesus Read* captures beautifully the importance of the prophets' message for us today. Listen carefully:

   In strange, complex images, the prophets present a wholly different view of the world. They offer hope, and something else: a challenge for us to live out the World as God Wants It in this life, right now. . . . What happens here on earth affects the future of the cosmos. From God's point of view, the future has already been determined, and the prophets spell out that future state in glowing detail: swords beaten into plowshares, a lamb recumbent beside a lion, a banquet feast. That is what God wants for this earth and that is what God will accomplish on this earth. The end is settled. What remains is whether we will live believing it.

   —Philip Yancey

   Why do you agree or disagree with this perspective? What difference might this perspective make to your life today?

Personal Journey: To Begin Now

Ironically, the seventeen most unread books of the Bible are the same books that give us the most complete picture of God's personality. With a passion that borders on the bizarre, the prophets proclaim to the human race that we matter to God. Over and over again, their urgent messages ring out to reveal a personal God who cares about every human being, who longs to be in relationship with us, and—above all— who loves us.

With this in mind, take some time now by yourself to consider the following questions.

1. Consider God's deep love for you—how he is always willing to forgive you, extend mercy to you, guide you. If he were to send a messenger—a prophet—to you as he did to the nations of Israel and Judah, what do you think he would say?

   a. How might God express his love in a way that is meaningful to you?

   b. What might God remind you he has done for you?

   c. How might God describe his greatest desires for your life or issue a word of warning?

2. In what way(s) can you express your thankfulness to God for his love and all that he has done for you?

3. In which area(s) of your life do you need to ask for God's forgiveness so that your relationship with him can be all that he desires it to be?

Personal Journey: To Do between Sessions

The startling actions and mythic visions of the prophets seem strange to us because the prophets are revealing to mortal humans a glimpse of God's cosmic viewpoint. The prophets seek to open our eyes to the world as God sees it, and that viewpoint is, at best, difficult for us to grasp. Their messages transcend time, speaking to the present as well as to the future. If we will listen, we will gain a vision of what God is ultimately doing in the world and will receive hope to endure the challenges of the present.

1. Make a list of the challenges you face in your life.

    a. Describe how these challenges appear from your viewpoint.

    b. From what you know of God and Scripture, how might God's viewpoint differ from yours?

c. What thoughts and feelings arise as you consider God's viewpoint?

2. How we approach the challenges of life makes a big difference. Philip Yancey has discovered that the prophets have a very important message for us regarding our approach:

> The prophets point us back to the present, yet ask us to live in the light of the future they image up. Can we trust their vision and accept it as the true reality of earth, despite all evidence to the contrary? Can we live now "as if" God is loving, gracious, merciful, and all-powerful? The prophets remind us that indeed God is and that history itself will one day bear that out. The World as It Is will become the World as God Wants It.

Take another look at the challenges of your life and evaluate each one in terms of how it might be different if you lived "as if" God is loving, gracious, merciful, and all-powerful.

a. In what way(s) might you change your approach to each challenge if you respond to it in light of the future God promises?

b. Do you truly believe that God reigns even though this world shows little evidence of that? Why?

c. Do you trust God enough to be able to rest in his powerful, loving embrace even though you live in dangerous, chaotic times? Explain what difference this will make in how you live.

d. Evaluate your desire to know God on an intimate, personal level and to take on his heart and passion.

Changing our perspective and approach is quite an adventure in faith. These questions cannot be answered easily and put aside. They should remain before us daily as we seek to know God and grow in our relationship with him.

Perspective

If only we could believe that our struggle really is against principalities and powers, if only we could believe that God will prove himself trustworthy and set right all that is wrong, if only we could demonstrate God's passion for justice and truth in this world—then, I think, the prophets will have accomplished their most urgent mission.

—Philip Yancey

Advance Echoes of a Final Answer

In a sense, all of Old Testament history serves as a preparation for Jesus, with the characters on its pages contributing a family, an identity, and a race for Jesus to be born into. What did God have in mind with the long, convoluted story of the Hebrews? The answer of the New Testament is unequivocal: Jesus is what God had in mind. He came to reconcile humanity to God by extending God's kingdom beyond the boundaries of race to the entire world.

—Philip Yancey

Questions to Think About

1. If someone were to ask you, "What does the Old Testament offer to Christians today?" or "Why should a Christian read the Old Testament?" what would you say?

2. In what way(s) has the Old Testament story and the way the Old Testament writers present it deepened your walk with God? Compare the benefits the Old Testament brings to your spiritual life with the contributions of the New Testament.

3. How would you describe the personality of God revealed in the Old Testament as compared to the New Testament? In what way(s) has your perception changed as a result of our study?

Video Presentation: "Advance Echoes of a Final Answer"

The Old and New Testaments: both are necessary

The Old Testament story: a longing for Jesus

Finding comfort in the Old Testament

Making the Old Testament our own

A testimony to God's timeless work

Video Highlights

1. In what ways do you see the Old and New Testaments complementing and completing one another?

2. Philip Yancey believes we "truly understand Jesus only by reading the Old Testament." In what way(s) do you see the Old Testament contributing to our understanding of Jesus?

3. This video portrays the Old Testament as having very personal overtones—being a source of comfort, an expression of the universal longings of the human heart. This perspective differs from a view of the Old Testament as being merely the history of the Hebrews and the source of the Ten Commandments. How have you traditionally viewed the Old Testament, and what are your responses to the perspective presented in this video?

Large Group Exploration: The Messiah—God's Answer to the Longings of His People

As he considers the Old Testament writings, Philip Yancey sees its writers expressing deep longings common to every human heart. These longings can be expressed in terms of three broad questions. He writes, "I return again and again to the Old Testament because it faces head-on these very questions. 'Do I matter?' 'Does God care?' 'Why doesn't God act?'"

The Old Testament writers, particularly the psalmists and prophets, eagerly pointed to a time when God would address these deep longings and answer the unanswered questions. They envisioned at least partial resolution to these longings at the coming of the Messiah. Let's consider some of these longings as they are brought to fruition in the person of Jesus.

1. Isaiah 42–53 records specific promises God gave in response to these longings and questions. First, let's look at some of the promises God made that boldly foretold the Incarnation—God's ultimate answer. Then, let's consider how the New Testament affirms that Jesus fulfilled God's promises.

Longings and Questions	What God Promised to Do	New Testament Affirmations that Jesus Fulfilled these Promises
Longing for justice	Isaiah 42:1–4:	Matthew 12:15–21; Acts 17:29–31:
Longing for God's presence with his people	Isaiah 42: 5–7:	Matthew 26:28; Luke 2:25–32:
Longing for God to act	Isaiah 43:19:	Mark 1:27; 2 Corinthians 5:17–19:

Longing for forgiveness and redemption	Isaiah 43:25; 44:21–23:	Matthew 26:27–28; Romans 8:1–4; 1 John 1:9:
Has God forsaken us?	Isaiah 49:14–16:	John 3:16; Romans 8:38; Hebrews 13:5:
Why do the wicked prosper?	Isaiah 51:4–8:	Matthew 13:40–43; 25:41–46; 2 Peter 3:10–13:

2. "Whenever I read straight through the Bible," Philip Yancey writes, "a huge difference between the Old and New Testaments comes to light. In the Old Testament I can find many expressions of doubt and disappointment.... In striking contrast, the New Testament Epistles contain little of this type of anguish. The problem of pain surely has not gone away ... Nevertheless, nowhere do I find the piercing question, Does God care? ... The reason for the change, I believe, is that Jesus answered that question for the witnesses who wrote the Epistles."

   Read Romans 5:1–8. In what way(s) do you recognize the difference Philip Yancey noted between the Old Testament perspective and the New Testament perspective?

Perspective

I have learned to love the Old Testament because it so poignantly expresses my own inner longings. I find in it a realism about human nature that is sorely absent from much smiley-face Christian propaganda. And yet the Old Testament writers, especially the psalmists and prophets, eagerly point ahead to a time when God has vowed to address those longings, to answer the questions that never go away.

—Philip Yancey

Small Group Exploration: Do We Matter to God?

Years ago the psalmist asked, "What is man that you are mindful of him?" (Psalm 8:4). Although we may word it differently, that question still echoes in the human heart. Each of us wants to know if we really matter to God, if God truly loves and cares for us as individuals. The coming of the Messiah, the birth of Jesus on this earth, answered that question with a resounding "yes!"

"In effect," Philip Yancey writes, "the holiday we celebrate as Christmas memorializes God's answer to the Hebrews' question, *Do we matter?* Here on earth, for thirty-three years, God experienced in flesh what it is like to be one of us. In the stories he told, and the people whose lives he touched, Jesus answered for all time that vexing question."

After breaking into groups of three to five, have someone in your group read the Scripture passage listed.

1. One way Jesus communicated God's love for us was through the parables he told. Read the following parables. In each case, how did Jesus show we matter to God?

   a. Luke 15:1–7

   b. Luke 15:11–24

2. It isn't enough to be told we matter; we long to see proof in action. Repeatedly, Jesus showed people who didn't matter to society that they mattered to God. What outstanding demonstration of this do we see in Matthew 8:1–3?

3. To show how very much we matter to him, what ultimate sacrifice did Jesus make for each of us? (See John 3:16; 1 John 4:10.)

4. When we are suffering or are in pain, it's easy to wonder if God still cares. Two instances in the Gospels especially show the compassionate, caring heart of God. How did Jesus respond in each instance?

   a. John 11:1–3, 17–19, 32–36

   b. Luke 19:41–44

Did You Know?

We *matter* to God. In a rare moment when he pulled back the curtain between seen and unseen worlds, Jesus said that angels rejoice when a single sinner repents. A solitary act on this speck of a planet reverberates throughout the cosmos.

—Philip Yancey

Group Discussion

1. The realism of the Old Testament—people's doubts, questions,
   struggles—first attracted Philip Yancey and then captured his attention. In what way(s) has God been changing your views of the Old
   Testament since we started this series? What has drawn you to value
   more highly the Old Testament?

2. After the Old Testament writings were completed, God was silent for
   four hundred years. Then he finally *acted* by sending the Messiah. In
   what ways does the coming of the Messiah affirm to you that you
   matter, that God cares, and that God does take action (albeit on his
   own timetable)?

3. Philip Yancey has come to believe that when we add Jesus to the Old Testament story, things fall into place differently than if we read the Old Testament without him. In what way(s) do you agree or disagree?

4. What excites you most about the opportunity to read and study more of the Old Testament as a result of what you have learned during this group study?

Perspective

To the question, *Why doesn't God act?* Jews and Christians have the same answer, with one crucial difference. Jews believe that God will act, by sending the Messiah. Christians believe that God has acted, by sending the Messiah, and will act once more, by sending him again, this time in power and glory, not in weakness and humility.

—Philip Yancey

Personal Journey: To Begin Now

The Old and New Testaments complement each other, and are, in fact, incomplete without the other. Jesus is the completion, the fulfillment, of the Old Testament promises. The Old Testament is essential to understanding Jesus and the New Testament.

With this in mind, take some time now by yourself to respond to the following questions.

1. Continuing to become more familiar with the Old Testament can open up whole new areas to us in our spiritual walk.

   a. What would be the benefits to you of continuing to search out and grow in your knowledge and understanding of the Old Testament?

   b. Describe some ways in which you will continue exploring the Old Testament during the days and weeks ahead. (These might include following a reading plan, using a concordance and/or study Bible to trace specific references Jesus made to the Old Testament, using a study Bible or other reference to better understand the Old Testament images Jesus used in his teachings, etc.)

c. What is your commitment to begin reading the Old Testament regularly?

2. Write down the Bible passages that mean a great deal to you. Are most of them from the Old Testament or New Testament? Why do you think you have chosen these passages?

Personal Journey

The Old Testament expresses our deepest longings and the questions that haunt our hearts. Although they at times were plagued by doubt and disappointment, the Old Testament writers still focus our eyes on the hope of the promises God has made in response to our longings. The realism and honesty of these writers as they waited for God to act provides comfort and encouragement to us as we, too, await the final unfolding of God's promises.

1. In which area(s) of your life right now do you need comfort? Make a list of any struggles, doubts, longings, discouragements, fears, and pain you are having a hard time coping with on your own.

   a. In what way(s) does the message that you matter to God, that he cares for you, and that he has (and will) take action impact your personal struggles and longings?

  b. What do you expect Jesus to do to meet you in your struggles and longings? How have you expressed those feelings to God?

2. Sometimes it is difficult for us to express our deepest feelings and needs to God. We may be too afraid or too weary to do so, but God still wants us to share our hearts with him. The Old Testament writers held nothing back when they opened their hearts to God. Sometimes, when we are incapable of expressing ourselves to God, *their* words express our thoughts exactly. Spend some time browsing the psalms. When you find a psalm that touches your heart, substitute details from your life into the psalm, and make it your own prayer to God.

Perspective

My father-in-law, Hunter Norwood, lived a rich, full life of eighty years. He sailed to South America as a missionary in 1942, built a house in the jungle by hand, founded a church and Bible Institute, and later returned to the U.S. to direct a mission organization. He was known by many as a Bible teacher *par excellence.* Eventually, due to cancer and a nerve-degenerating disease, he could no longer teach the Bible, but he continued to study it faithfully each day.

As his illness progressed, Hunter's world shrank to the size of a hospital bed, which he rarely left. Those of us who knew him well know that the last few years of his life were by far the hardest. Opponents of his faith had stoned him in Columbia. He had coped with alligators, boa constrictors, and piranhas in Peru. He had raised six daughters in two different cultures. But none of these compared to the difficulties of lying in bed all day, his body defying his every command, waiting to die. Toward the end, it took all his effort to accomplish the simple acts of swallowing and breathing.

It is hard to maintain a spirit of joy and victory when your body rebels against you, when you must call for help to drink a glass of water or blow your nose. As we are inclined to do, Hunter went through a crisis of faith during those last few years, but he never stopped relating to God. Until the day he could no longer hold a pen, he recorded a journal of his wrestling with God. As I studied the hundreds of entries in that journal, I found only nine entries referring to New Testament texts. All the others are from the Old Testament.

The wavering yet rock-solid faith Hunter found in the Old Testament sustained him when nothing else could. Even at his most doubt-filled moments, he took comfort in the fact that some of God's favorites had battled the very same demons. He learned that the arms of the Lord are long and wrap around those he loves. I am glad that, in those dark days, Hunter Norwood had the Old Testament to fall back on.

—Philip Yancey

We want to hear from you. Please send your comments about this book to us in care of zreview@zondervan.com. Thank you.

ZONDERVAN.com/
AUTHORTRACKER
follow your favorite authors